"I'm Sorry to Hear That…"

Real-Life Responses to Patients' 101 Most Common Complaints About Health Care

by Susan Keane Baker & Leslie Bank

Published by:
Fire Starter Publishing
913 Gulf Breeze Parkway, Suite 6
Gulf Breeze, FL 32561
Phone: 850-934-1099
Fax: 850-934-1384
www.firestarterpublishing.com

Cover design by Cassandra Henze

ISBN: 978-0-9749986-5-7

Library of Congress Control Number: 2008941136

Printed in the United States of America

FOREWORD

This is a timely book.

The growing burden of health care costs is commoditizing what was once taken for granted as a semi sacred social domain. As health care takes an increasing chunk out of the GNP (and our individual pocketbooks), the public is coming to demand value for its money. This means greater attention to the quality of all aspects of care—whether technical or personal. The patient/consumer is steadily recognizing that the hand that heals can indeed be bitten—both through demands for higher quality care and through complaints about care that fails to meet rising standards. And the patient/ consumer can bite even harder. Dissatisfaction with care (not outright error) underlies most malpractice suits.

With the rise of public "report cards" on hospital quality, plus various "Top 100" hospital or physician lists, the public inevitably will increasingly take it for granted that providers differ in the quality of facilities, expertise, and personal care they offer. Expectations of service excellence will increase. The confidence that "it's okay to complain" while still under care will grow. Complaint management (a.k.a. "service recovery") will become a key strategy for risk management, customer retention, and word of mouth marketing. It's old hat now that dissatisfied patients have an impact on hospital reputation and bottom line. Moreover, dissatisfied patients are more likely to be less cooperative and communicative while still under care.

On the other hand, we know that when complaints and service failures are directly addressed and remedied, the result is less litigious, more satisfied, cooperative, and supportive patients and families. This being said, it's often difficult for conscientious, harried staff to respond appropriately, on the spot, to an irate patient. Staff can be defensive—both when they are directly responsible for a glitch and when they had nothing to do with causing it. What to say? How to apologize without assuming or casting blame? How do you suggest a remedy for issues you don't control?

Bank and Baker's book provides ample answers to these questions. Across a wide spectrum of patient and family complaints, the authors offer thoughtful responses, couched in language that soothes while offering hope of a remedy. The book's great strength lies in its going beyond apologies—although these, too, are instructive—to practical solutions. Take for example the patient who complains that the home care nurse failed to show up. Here's the "apology":

"I'm sorry to hear that. Let me look at your record. Our notes indicate we have made two attempts to visit you and we've tried to call you. I'm glad you called us. Let's recheck the information we have on file and get your first visit scheduled."

Lots of things are communicated here. The staff member acknowledges the issue, indicates the patient's role in the service failure, then neatly compliments and rewards the patient by saying, "I'm glad you called," and ends by scheduling a specific revisit.

Everyone who deals with patients and their families will find this book useful. Bank and Baker empower the reader by suggesting effective ways of immediately responding to—and resolving—common patient dissatisfiers. There should be a copy on every unit and departmental shelf for quick reference.

Irwin Press, Ph.D.
Founder, Press Ganey Associates

TABLE OF CONTENTS

Complaints do not always fit into neat categories, but we have organized these 101 complaints into general compartments in order to help you understand how best to respond:

A complaint about **ACCESS** reveals a patient's need to obtain or preserve services in spite of perceived barriers. An effective response will reassure the patient that services will be received.

An **ENVIRONMENTAL** complaint reveals a patient's dissatisfaction with comfort, cleanliness, sense of privacy and well-being. Although these may seem more like hospitality issues, an effective response will establish a patient's sense of safety and confidence in his or her surroundings.

In sharp contrast to the clinical aspects of health care are the processes and people who deliver the service. A complaint about **SERVICE QUALITY** reveals a patient's feelings about being devalued and not treated like an important customer. An effective response will tell the patient that he or she is the most important part of your job.

Patients need to understand and participate in their care, and trust that their care will be safe and beneficial. A **QUALITY OF CARE** complaint reveals a patient's lessening confidence and emotional comfort with his or her clinical care. An effective response will be reassuring, respectful, and empowering.

One might say all complaints have a **COMMUNICATION** component; however, sometimes it is simply a matter of how we speak or write instructions, hold a conversation, or ignore cultural norms. An effective response will acknowledge communication failure with a promise of improvement.

BILLING is the final dimension of care. A patient's final opinion about his or her experience can be altered by poor billing practices such as inaccuracies and undecipherable messages. An effective response will re-establish confidence in the health care services received and trust in the business side of the enterprise.

Successful service recovery begins with understanding what a complaint really represents.

Complaints do not always fit into neat categories, but we have organized these 101 complaints into general compartments in order to help you understand how best to respond:

A complaint about **ACCESS** reveals a patient's need to obtain or preserve services in spite of perceived barriers. An effective response will reassure the patient that services will be received.

An **ENVIRONMENTAL** complaint reveals a patient's dissatisfaction with comfort, cleanliness, sense of privacy and well-being. Although these may seem more like hospitality issues, an effective response will establish a patient's sense of safety and confidence in his or her surroundings.

In sharp contrast to the clinical aspects of health care are the processes and people who deliver the service. A complaint about **SERVICE QUALITY** reveals a patient's feelings about being devalued and not treated like an important customer. An effective response will tell the patient that he or she is the most important part of your job.

Patients need to understand and participate in their care, and trust that their care will be safe and beneficial. **A QUALITY OF CARE** complaint reveals a patient's lessening confidence and emotional comfort with his or her clinical care. An effective response will be reassuring, respectful, and empowering.

One might say all complaints have a **COMMUNICATION** component; however, sometimes it is simply a matter of how we speak or write instructions, hold a conversation, or ignore cultural norms. An effective response will acknowledge communication failure with a promise of improvement.

BILLING is the final dimension of care. A patient's final opinion about his or her experience can be altered by poor billing practices such as inaccuracies and undecipherable messages. An effective response will re-establish confidence in the health care services received and trust in the business side of the enterprise.

Successful service recovery begins with understanding what a complaint really represents.

The icon(s) accompanying each complaint indicate where the problem is likely to occur or be addressed. The key is:

Home care setting

Hospital setting

Physician practice/other outpatient setting

We can't give you a single response that will work for every patient in every situation. Our goal is to give you confidence in your ability to respond to a patient's complaint in a way that preserves, and even enhances, your relationship. In addition, your understanding of issues that cause patients to complain will be strengthened by reading this guide.

If you've ever wished for specific responses to defuse tense situations, this guide is for you.

Leslie Bank &
Susan Keane Baker

1

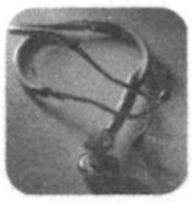

I called my doctor's office over and over, and they never called me back.

I'm sorry to hear that and I'd be happy to help. Please give me some details so I can try to prevent this from happening again.

I'm so sorry. It's hard to wait for a return call. How can I help you?

I'm sorry to hear that. Is there something I can help you with? If not, I can arrange a specific time for the doctor to call you.

2

What do you mean, you can't schedule a mammogram for four months? I'll have you know I am a very close friend of the president of the hospital. Jack and I belong to the same country club, and when I tell him about this, there'll be hell to pay. What's your name and what's your supervisor's name?

I'm sorry our schedule is so full. My name is Jane Smith and my supervisor's name is Suzanne Doria. We have several sites that provide mammography. They may have earlier openings. Would any of these other locations work for you so we can get you in sooner?

I'm sorry. Would you like me to call you if we have a cancellation? We might have a cancellation at any time, and although there are several names already on the cancellation list, we often call everyone on the list trying to find someone who can take a last-minute opening. My name is Jane and I hope we can resolve this to your satisfaction.

Mrs. (patient's name), my name is Jane Smith and I'm happy to help. We see patients for mammograms until 9:00 p.m. Would you be willing to have an appointment at 9:30 p.m. one evening? Perhaps one of our technicians will be willing to work late so we can squeeze you in sooner.

3

I expected my home care to begin three days ago. No one has come yet. My doctor said you'd be here already!

I'm sorry. I hear how upset you are because your service hasn't started yet. Your record indicates that you are scheduled for your first nursing visit tomorrow. Are you okay? Tell me what's happening.

I'm sorry to hear that. Let me look at your record. Our notes indicate we have made two attempts to visit you and we've tried to call you. I'm glad you called us. Let's recheck the information we have on file and get your first visit scheduled.

I'm sorry you've waited so long. We should have called you to give you the schedule for your visits. We'll be at your home between noon and one o'clock today. We're all set to begin your therapy. I'll call you later in the afternoon to see how your first visit went.

When I arrived for my appointment, they told me the doctor was out of town. Can you believe that?

I'm terribly sorry you weren't notified. Would you like to see another practitioner today, or would you rather reschedule with your regular doctor? Did you take the bus to get here? When you're ready to leave, I'm going to call a taxi and pay for your trip home. And I'll give you a taxi voucher for your next appointment, too, because we are sorry this happened.

I'm sorry this happened. Let's make another appointment at a time that's convenient for you. We should have notified you, and I will speak with our office staff. Is there anything I can do for you right now?

I'm so sorry. You are scheduled for lab tests, so we can at least get those done. And if you can come in at 8 tomorrow morning, the doctor will see you before our office opens at 8:30.

I don't understand why you can't see me without a referral. Can't you see I'm in pain?

I'm sorry you're in pain; let me call your doctor's office immediately.

I'm so sorry. I wish it were different. If we see you without a referral, your insurance company will not cover any of today's charges. We tell you this because we don't want you to be surprised when your insurance company rejects your claim and we bill you for the visit.

I'm sorry. We can see you without a referral if you plan to pay the bill yourself. Is that an option for you?

You lost my paperwork and, as a result, you're saying I can't be seen today?

I'm sorry that happened. Let me see how we can fix this right away. Who is your doctor?

I'm sorry. I don't see your name here, but sometimes mistakes happen. I'll call your doctor's office to see if they can fax the paperwork to us right away.

I'm sorry. Let's take a few minutes together so I can get all the necessary information about you, and then we'll go from there.

There aren't enough parking spaces for the disabled.

I'm sorry to hear that. When are you coming next? I'll be happy to arrange special parking for you next time. Would you like to write a note to our safety committee about your experience? Your comments will really make a difference.

I'm sorry. I know how difficult parking can be. I hope you won't experience this again, but if you do, please tell the security guard. He'll help you find a solution or let the garage attendant know you are having a problem. I'll remind them about what to do in this situation.

I'm sorry for your difficulty. If this continues to be a problem, I can arrange to meet you at the entrance and help you find a spot. Here is my business card; feel free to call me anytime.

My mother has been waiting for a bed in a nursing home/long-term care facility for months. When will she be able to get in? She is no longer able to stay at home, but we do not want to her to go to just any facility.

I'm sorry it's been so long. Let me check to see where she is on the facility's waiting list. It's hard to predict when a room will become available, but I will call and find out as much information as I can.

I'm sorry. I can see how concerned you are for your mother. What would your family like to do if a bed doesn't become available relatively soon at her first choice? We may face a problem if your home care services run out. We'll plan a family meeting with your social worker as soon as possible.

I'm sorry to hear that. We are all concerned about her. I will check with the facility to get the best information on when a bed will be available; then I will review her home services to see how much longer we are able to provide care. Then we'll talk again to review our options. Please consider us resources and partners with you in this.

I was told to be here at 7:00 a.m. and I wasn't taken back until 10:00 a.m. My time is valuable too, you know!

I'm very sorry no one told you what was happening or explained to you why we needed you here so early. We should always keep you informed. Is there anything I can do for you right now?

I'm sorry; we should have done much better than that. I'm going to ask about why this happened. Would you like me to let you know what I learn?

I agree with you; your time is valuable. Please let me know when your next visit is scheduled, and I'll check on you while you're here.

Others who came after me were seen before me. What's going on? That's not fair!

I'm sorry. Sometimes people are waiting for different tests or services. Let me find out what's happening.

I'm sorry that happened. We try to see patients in order of appointment, not arrival. Some people are not as conscientious as you are about arriving early for their appointments.

I'm sorry. It's hard to wait. Let me check for you about how much longer it should be. Please don't hesitate to ask at the desk if you feel something's not right.

11

When am I going to get a room? I've been waiting here for hours. I can't take this another minute! This stretcher is very uncomfortable. What's wrong with this Emergency Room?

Oh my goodness, I'll get an update for you right now and make you as comfortable as I can—how can I help?

I'm sorry. Every minute must feel like forever. The plan is for you to move to 7 North. Let me find out what's happening. I'll be right back.

I'm sorry to hear that. I'm going to check with your doctor to see if you can have some food. If you can eat, is there a snack I can fix for you? Is there anyone you need to call? I can bring a phone over to you. Would another pillow make you a little more comfortable?

12

I don't have enough help at home. I need more hours of help. The case manager has reduced my hours. I need those hours because I'm elderly and need someone to be here to help me.

I'm sorry. We'll review your chart and insurance coverage and see what we can do. What do you feel you need? Let's make a list and look at your needs one at a time.

I'm sorry to hear how worried you are. Have you spoken with your doctor about this? Your insurance provides a certain level of assistance. Beyond that, patients need to accept financial responsibility for additional hours and/or services. We can figure this all out together.

I'm sorry to hear you're not getting all the help you want. I've checked your orders and you are receiving the maximum services your health coverage allows. Perhaps we can explore other community services for you.

13

I don't want to see an intern or resident. I want a real doctor.

Some patients are not aware that house staff are real doctors. All interns and residents have a medical degree. It's the number of years of experience that determines whether someone is an intern or resident. And interns and residents work under the supervision of your attending physician.

I'm sorry. If you prefer not to have interns or residents see you, we can arrange that. However, before you decide, I'd like to explain some of the benefits of being cared for by our house staff doctors.

I'm sorry to hear that. All interns and residents are real doctors with medical degrees, and our hospital accepts only highly qualified medical graduates. Please tell me more—has something happened that has upset you?

14

I am feeling too ill to leave the hospital. I'm not ready to go home. I need another day.

I'm sorry you're not feeling well. Does your doctor know you're not feeling well enough to go? I can call her for you. You have the right to protest your discharge from the hospital. I'll make sure you have all the information you need if you decide to do that.

I'm sorry to hear that. Many people don't feel 100 percent before they go home. Has anyone discussed with you what you need in terms of medications, home care, and information about what to expect? Let's talk about what would help you feel better about being home.

I'm sorry; it sounds like you're worried about going home. We always call our patients the day after discharge to see how they are. When you get home, if anything is wrong, I want you to call me. This is my card, with my direct extension on it, so you can call me anytime. Please let me know how you are.

15

My home care stops next week, and I don't think I'll be okay. I'm scared about being alone all the time.

I'm sorry to hear that. We're obligated to make sure you have a safe discharge from our services. Would you like me to help you make a list of all the things you're worried about? Your nurse is due to visit you tomorrow. I'll give her the list, and she will go over everything with you.

I'm sorry. We don't want you to be afraid. Your nurse, social worker and therapist are impressed with your progress and feel you handle yourself very well. If you need help after discharge, we're just a phone call away.

I'm sorry you feel uncertain, but it's normal to feel that way. We are confident you're ready, and your insurance benefits have been used up. Let's consider your options. One would be to ask you to pay privately for additional services, and I could give you an estimate of what the costs would be. Another option would be for us to check in with you by telephone each day during your first week after discharge. Usually, we call patients a week after discharge to see if everything is okay, but we could check on you more often if that would be helpful.

The tray table/end table/chair/piece of furniture is broken, and no one is doing anything about it.

I'm so sorry. Let me take it from your room right now. I'll find another one and bring it in.

Oh dear, that's not good. May I use your phone to call Engineering and ask them to bring a new one right away? I'll put some masking tape across this one so no one else will use it. I'll check back in an hour to make sure this has been taken care of.

I'm sorry no one has come to take it away. We have a new service where you can call our Facilities Department directly for any room problems. Before we call, is there anything else we should tell them?

My room hasn't been cleaned in days. No one has emptied my wastebasket and no one has changed my linens. What kind of a place is this?

I'm sorry to hear that. Let me ask someone from Environmental Services to come see you. I can empty your wastebasket right now. Because this has been a problem for several days, I'll ask our Director of Environmental Services to visit you as soon as possible.

I'm sorry. Let's start by changing your linens right now. Would you like me to get an extra wastebasket for you? Let's make a checklist of the things needing attention so we fix everything.

I'm sorry to hear that. What needs special attention today? Our staff try to clean when patients are out of the room so they don't disturb you or your visitors. I'll ask your Environmental Services Associate to leave a note on your whiteboard, so you know someone was here to clean your room.

18

The nurse didn't bring me extra gauze and bandages. I used to get lots of supplies and now I'm not getting anything.

I'm sorry you didn't get extra supplies. I'll make a note in your chart that this is important to you, check what your insurance will cover, and be sure we give you as much as we can.

I'm sorry things have changed. You're absolutely right. We used to bring a lot of extra supplies with us. Unfortunately, there are limits on what we can do these days. We can bring only what most patients need until the next visit. If we leave extra supplies for you, the next patients would not have the supplies needed for their care. I'm sorry we can't be as free with extra supplies as we used to be.

I'm sorry. Do you have enough to last you until next Tuesday? Are you running short? Let's go over the technique again on how—and how often—to do your dressing change. I want to make sure you have what you need.

19

The bath seat was too big for our bathroom, and we have told them, but they keep sending us the wrong one.

I'm sorry to hear that. I'd be upset too. Please give me as much information as you can. I'm going to investigate and make things right for you.

Oh my, I'm so sorry. Has anyone explained to you why this has happened? We work with this equipment vendor exclusively, and they promise us excellent service. I'll call the manager and straighten things out. I'm sure she will want to contact you to apologize as well.

I'm sorry. We need to fix this quickly so you are safe and confident. First, I want to be sure we have ordered the correct item. Then, I'll follow up to get it to you and make sure this doesn't happen to someone else. Thank you for your patience. I'll call you on Tuesday to make sure you've received your bath seat.

When I went to pick up the equipment for my husband, it was filthy.

I'm sorry. That shouldn't be. Let's make an exchange this afternoon. Would it be convenient for you to drop it off today? If that's not possible, I'll send someone to pick it up.

I'm sorry that happened. If you've already cleaned it yourself, I apologize and thank you. There's no excuse for poorly prepared equipment and I'll make sure we check everything more carefully before we release items. Is there something I can do for you or your husband right now?

I am so sorry and embarrassed to hear this. We'll visit you with a replacement today.

There's always something missing from my tray.

I'm sorry to hear that. What do you need? I'm going to call Food and Nutrition Services and ask them to deliver it right away. I'll check back with you in thirty minutes to make sure it's arrived.

I'm sorry that happened. We want you to enjoy your meals, so let me make this right for you immediately. What's missing? I'll run over to the kitchen and bring it right back.

I want to call your dietician so she can double-check your diet orders with you. But right now, let's call the Food Service Hotline. I'll write the hotline number on your whiteboard, so if this happens again, you can get help quickly. Or call me just as you did today. I'll stop by tomorrow at lunchtime and double-check to make sure everything you need is on your tray.

The food is tasteless. The tea is never hot, the cereal is too thick, and the toast is soggy.

I'm sorry to hear you're not enjoying your meal. I'll check your nutrition orders and ask the dietician to visit you. She may be able to suggest some alternatives. Shall I make you a cup of hot tea right now?

I'm sorry. Good nutrition is important to your recovery. We have some snacks on the unit. Is there something I can get you? I could make you some fresh toast or a sandwich.

Even though some special diets are very strict, our Food & Nutrition team strives to provide tasty food. I'm going to ask your nutritionist if there are spices we can use to add flavor to your meals. What do you use at home?

I couldn't find a parking place. There's never enough parking, so I got a ticket.

I know it's frustrating when there are no free spaces. Would you like me to schedule your next appointment later in the afternoon when it's easier to find a space?

I'm sorry you received a parking ticket. We have an employee parking garage with special rates for patients. I can give you this information to make it easier for you next time. Also, we do have valet parking. There's no charge, and no tipping is allowed.

or

Many patients are happy to find out that the charge for the valet to park your car is only $_____.

I'm so sorry. I don't know if it will help, but I'm happy to write a letter for you explaining our parking challenges. That might help with the ticket. Next time, give me a call before you leave home, and I'll make sure there is someone at the entrance to help you find a spot.

24

Your signs are lousy. I've been wandering around for hours. How does anyone find their way around this place?

I'm sorry; where do you need to go? I'd be happy to take you there. Let me show you the way.

I'm sorry. We are working on improving our signs. What was most confusing? Can I escort you somewhere right now?

If this should happen again, please ask anyone wearing a nametag for help. They will be happy to take you to your destination or find another employee going in the same direction to escort you.

The therapist is wearing aftershave and it's making me sick to my stomach. Some of the nursing staff is wearing perfume, and I am allergic to perfume.

I'm sorry. I'll let them know it bothers you. Our service standards require us not to wear colognes or other scents. I'll remind everyone.

I'm sorry. How are you feeling right now? Could I get you some crackers to settle your stomach? I'll make sure this doesn't happen again. Right now I'm going to ask the technician to go to the staff lounge and wash up.

I'm sorry and thank you for telling me. I'll remind all our staff. People are sensitive to smells especially when they don't feel well. Your comfort is very important to us. Please let me know if anything like this happens again.

26

I'm freezing. Can you do anything about the temperature?

I'm sorry you're cold. Let me adjust the thermostat and get an extra blanket for you.

Oh dear. We're very fortunate to have individual room thermostats, so I can warm things up for you right now. Would you like me to show you how you can control your room temperature yourself?

I'll get you a robe and find out if we can do anything about it. The boilers are adjusted seasonally, so when the weather is unexpectedly cold, it can take a few days for the building to warm up. By that time, it may be warm outside again, and then the building becomes too hot. Would a cup of tea help, along with the robe?

I can't sleep with all the noise around here.

I'm sorry. That's terrible. I will remind the staff to be as quiet as possible. Sometimes we forget. We have been working on reducing noise levels, especially at night. I will definitely let the team know we still have room for improvement.

I'm so sorry. Is it voices, equipment, doors, or a combination of many noises? Next week, we are putting rubber coatings on the wheels of all our carts. That will cut down on equipment noise, but we need to work on the human side too! Some patients prefer to close their door.

I'm sorry you aren't able to sleep. We have a program called SHHH!, which stands for "Silent hospitals help healing." Do you have some suggestions about how we can make it less noisy at night? I'll share your ideas with our night staff.

28

You lost my cell phone/dentures/belongings/ wheelchair/glasses/prosthesis.

I'm so sorry to hear that. That's terrible! Let me look into this right away. When did you last see your property? Let's see if we can trace this back and find out what happened.

I'm sorry to hear that. Do you have any idea where they might be? I will start looking right away, and I'll check with staff in all the places you have been. Let's hope your belongings are safely waiting someplace.

I'm very sorry; you must be upset. I would be too. When was the last time you remember having them? I want to do everything we can to find your property. I'll do my best for you.

I hate my roommate. He has too many visitors. I can't get any rest with all the talking.

I'm sorry to hear that and I understand why you feel this way. The open visiting policy is helpful for some, but we need to manage our two-visitor rule better, because you aren't getting the rest you need.

I'm sorry. Have you spoken with your roommate about this? I'll try to keep a closer eye on things and ask his visitors to lower their voices and spend more time visiting in the lounge. I'll talk to your roommate and try to explain your difficulty, if you'd like me to.

I'm sorry. Let me see if we can transfer you to another room. I'll ask the nurses if there is a quieter room available. Most of our patients have only a few visitors.

The person you've assigned to me is stealing from me.

I'm so sorry to hear that. We will investigate this right away and assign another staff member until we can be sure what happened. We are very serious about protecting the safety of our patients and their property.

I'm sorry. Please don't worry; we'll get to the bottom of this. It's very important to us that you feel respected and your property is safe.

I'm very distressed to hear that. Please tell me what happened and what's missing. I'd like all the details so I can investigate this immediately. I'll send a different staff member tomorrow so you don't have to worry.

I could hear everything about my roommate's condition. Now that I know what's wrong with her, I need to get out of here!

Oh my, I'm sorry to hear that you're concerned. Let me see whether a transfer can be arranged quickly for you.

I'm sorry you overheard information that alarmed you. I want to assure you that we wouldn't place you with a contagious patient. Contagious patients are always given special rooms to prevent their infections from spreading to others. We call it "isolation." Does that help? If not, I'll see what I can do to find you another room, but it may take me a little time.

I'm so sorry. I can't discuss another patient's condition with you, so I can't be specific, but please don't be alarmed. We have very strict infection control rules, and we would never jeopardize your safety. Would you like to meet with our infection control specialist? She'd be delighted to meet with you.

32

I heard the doctors talking about me in the hallway.

I'm sorry—that should never happen. I'm glad you told me so I can remind everyone that all discussions need to take place in private areas. Would you like me to speak with your doctors about this?

I'm sorry. Tell me what happened. I'll investigate right away and I will make sure the residents know this is not acceptable. Can you tell me more? It's very important that we protect your privacy.

I'm sorry this happened to you. We have a private consultation area for discussions like that. I'll remind everyone to be careful about hallway conversations.

I closed my door and people entered without knocking. Even though there was a "do not disturb" sign on the door, staff barged right in.

I'm sorry to hear that. Our service standards require knocking before entering. I will review this with the staff.

Sometimes staff feel the "do not disturb" signs are for visitors only. I'll remind them to always knock first.

I'm sorry; I'll remind everyone that it's important to knock before entering. And, after they knock, they need to wait for your answer. Thank you for letting me know.

34

Why are you putting my Social Security number on this? Who's going to see it?

We need to include your Social Security number on the form in order to file your insurance claim. The only people who will see your form are those involved with processing the claim.

I can appreciate your concern. Your Social Security number assists us in making sure your record is maintained accurately. Even if someone else has your same name, the Social Security number provides a check to make sure your medical records contain only your information.

I'm sorry this worries you. We have significant security safeguards to protect your information. Every employee signs a pledge to protect your privacy. Your number is not shared with anyone except your insurance company, unless you authorize us to do so.

35

This gown doesn't give me enough privacy. I feel exposed and embarrassed in this gown.

I'm sorry; I'll fix this right away for you. I can add a second gown and double them so that one is worn in the front and the other in the back, and you'll be covered.

Thank you for letting me know. Would you like a different size? I'll get one for you right away so we can see what's best for you.

I'm sorry about that. Let me get a robe (or pajama bottoms) for you right away. Would you prefer to wear your own clothes/pajamas/nightgown?

36

There was no privacy at the desk when I was registering. Everyone heard my business!

Your privacy is very important to us, and I'm sorry to hear you didn't feel yours was respected. I'd like to tell the staff how you felt and what you think they should have done differently.

I'm so sorry and thank you for letting me know. I'm going to speak with our supervisor and ask him to put this as the first topic on our staff meeting agenda.

That's a very open spot and we're working on ways to make it more private. Next time, please ask the staff member to lower his voice, or ask for a piece of paper so you can write down your answers. I'm very sorry.

What's going on with my mom? No one is telling me anything.

I'm sorry. You are right to be concerned for your mother. Let's go in and sit with her and talk about your questions.

I'm sorry to hear that. I hear your concern about your mom. You probably know about the federal privacy rules. I just need to check with your mother to see what information I can share with you. Has your mother appointed a Health Care Agent in case there is a time she cannot direct her care or give permission to release information? This might be a good time to talk with her about that. I could help you do this, if you'd like.

You sound very concerned about your mom. I'm not able to discuss her patient information without her permission. Could you ask her to give me a call so she can tell me what information I can share with you?

38

Medical information was given to my spouse without my permission.

I'm sorry to hear that. What happened? We want to, and are obligated to, protect your privacy.

I'm very sorry. We care about the privacy of your health information. I will investigate and let you know what I learn. First, please tell me what has happened.

I'm sorry to hear that happened. I know your spouse is always with you and has been present in most of our discussions. Please help me understand so we can make sure to do exactly as you wish when it comes to your health information.

39

They told me my doctor would see me at 8:00 a.m. It's now 10:00. My daughter drove me and she has to leave in a few minutes to go to work.

I'm so sorry about this. Would it make sense for your daughter to head off to work and we'll give you something to eat? Could she come back at lunchtime for you?

Oh dear. I'm so sorry. What can we arrange right now that would be best for both of you?

I'm sorry to hear that. An emergency this morning did put us behind. What can we do to help? Could we call a taxi for you after you meet with the doctor? Would an evening appointment this week help? Would your daughter want us to call her boss and explain about the emergency? Would you like to see the physician assistant instead? I could ask him to see you immediately.

I didn't get back to my room from the x-ray hallway for hours. You forgot about me!

I'm so sorry. That must have been very uncomfortable. Can I do something for you right now?

I'm sorry. That should never happen. I will ask the head of Transportation Services to speak to you personally. I'm sure she'll want to hear about this.

I'm so sorry. We need to do much better. I'll check to see which tests are scheduled for you today and personally make sure your transportation is on time.

41

It took forever for anyone to answer my call bell. To make matters worse, once the nurse finally showed up, she said she'd be right back, and she never returned.

Oh my, I'm sorry to hear that. We need to respond quickly after you call. First, I'll make sure your call bell is working; then I'll let your nurse manager know. We plan to start hourly rounds this week with all our patients, so whether you ring the call bell or not, someone will be checking in on you more frequently. This should help a lot.

I'm sorry to hear that. I know that whenever you're waiting, time passes very slowly. This is especially true in a hospital. What can I do for you right now?

I'm sorry—we're working on shortening our response time. Let me speak with your nurses and see what's happening. Is there anything I can do for you?

The home care aide is always late.

I'm sorry to hear that. Let's try this. I will ask your aide to call into the office when she arrives at your home. Making her accountable for her time should help this situation.

I'm sorry. Sometimes traffic, or a delay with an earlier patient, means that the aide is unavoidably late. Many aides use public transportation, so we ask patients to allow a thirty-minute grace period. We appreciate your patience, but it's still frustrating for you. How often does this happen?

I'm sorry to hear that. I'll speak with your aide about punctuality, and check in with you in a few days to see if there's been improvement. I hope you'll call me anytime you have questions or comments about our services.

43

I requested a copy of my medical record a month ago and haven't received it. When I asked last week, the clerk told me they were still looking for it. I know my rights and I want my chart.

I'm sorry to hear that. We keep a record of these requests and track their progress. If you can give me just a few moments, I should be able to tell you exactly what's happening.

I'm very sorry. You are correct. You do have a right to a copy of your chart. Sometimes a chart gets signed out for one reason or another, and it takes us time to locate it. We have not been able to find yours. We have a process to begin reconstructing your record. To get started, can we set up an appointment for you to come in at no charge and have a physical?

I'm sorry this is taking so long. You should have had your chart by now. I'll do everything I can to fix this. The hospital has begun putting all patient records on computer by optical imaging. Soon, when you want your record, we'll just press the "print" button. But for now, I know it's really hard to wait. I hope I will know something later today. Where can I reach you?

I wait and wait for someone to help me to the bathroom.

Oh dear, I'm sorry this happens. Let me help you right now, and I will let all your caregivers know. I'll stop by more frequently to see if you need help.

I'm sorry to hear that—we don't want that to happen. We need to improve. If it's all right with you, I will talk with your nurses. We need to give you the help you need when you need it.

Have you met your Nurse Manager? He should know about this so he can remind his staff that helping you to the bathroom is a priority.

I dropped off a form two weeks ago to be completed, and it's still not done. I need it right away!

I'm sorry. I know you dropped off the form. Let me check your chart and see if it's been completed.

I'm sorry. Can you wait a few minutes while I find out where your form is? I'd like to take care of it now. I'll be right back.

I'm sorry you don't have the form yet. I'm sure it will be completed by Wednesday. Would you like me to call your school/employer to explain that we are the reason for the delay, not you?

46

I had to wait while staff joked and talked about their personal business. They were loud, rude, and disrespectful. I just stood there. / The agency worker did not show up at my home when she was supposed to, and when I called the agency, the person I talked to was very rude. / The staff was rude to my family. / The receptionist was rude and inconsiderate.

I'm sorry to hear that and thank you for telling me. We will not tolerate rude behavior and this will be corrected. You've made a difference for other patients, too. Thank you.

There is no excuse for anyone to be rude. I'm sorry you experienced that. I will speak to him and tell him how his behavior affected you. Is that okay?

I'm very sorry. We have strict standards of behavior for all employees, and I'm disturbed to hear about your experience. I will investigate and take corrective action. Please accept my apologies. Is there anything I can do for you right now?

47

You're good, but no one else helps me.

Thank you for the compliment, but I'm sorry you don't think they're helpful. Please tell me more so I can decide what I need to do.

I'm sorry. Can you give me some specific suggestions about how others can help you better? I want you to have confidence in all of us.

I'm sorry to hear that. It's important that the staff understands how you're feeling. I'd like to bring our manager in so you can explain this to her. We need to change this for you.

48

The nurse calls me "sweetie" or "dearie," and I don't appreciate it.

I'm sorry to hear that. How would you like to be addressed? I will note it on your preference card, and I will make sure your nurse uses your proper name from now on.

One of our service standards is to always address our patients by their last names unless they ask us not to. I will remind all staff that this standard applies to everyone.

I'm sorry and I apologize. Does she know you feel this way? I'd be happy to speak with her, if you'd like.

49

The staff talks down to me and treats me like I'm a dope.

I'm sorry to hear that. Can you tell me a bit more, please? I'd like to understand what's happening and how we can improve.

Oh dear. I'm sorry. What do they say to make you feel this way? How can I make it better? I'd be glad to sit with you when staff visits to see how things go.

I'm sorry; that's not good. You must feel badly about that. What can we do differently to make this better for you?

50

The home care aide always leaves early.

I'm sorry to hear that. According to your record, your aide is supposed to visit you for one hour, twice a week. Please give me more details. How much time is she spending with you?

I'm sorry. It's very important you receive the services we promised. I'm going to ask your aide to call me when she is ready to leave your home.

I'm sorry to hear that. We expect all our staff to work professionally and thoroughly. Please give me more information so I am able to discuss this with your aide. I want to be sure you are receiving all the care you need.

51

The nurse wouldn't remove her shoes when she came into my apartment/home, until I screamed.

I'm sorry that happened. We feel strongly about our role as a guest in your home. We want to respect your preferences whenever possible. I'll speak with your nurse and make a note in your chart so that everyone who visits you remembers to take off their shoes.

I'm sorry. Our agency holds our staff to high standards of respecting our patients' cultures and preferences. It is your home. Would you like me to speak with your nurse about this? Again, I'm sorry this was upsetting for you.

I'm very sorry. We want to meet your requests whenever possible. I will remind all your caregivers that you prefer people to remove their shoes each time they enter your home.

52

Are you telling me there's no private room available? I do not want a roommate. Do you know how much money my family donates to this hospital every year?

I'm sorry. Unfortunately, there are no private rooms at the moment. What I can do is put your name on the priority list so when a private room becomes available, we'll move you rather than assign it to a new patient. I'll keep you posted.

I'm sorry; I wish I had a private room to give you. Everyone here is grateful for your family's generosity. As soon as a room is available, we'll move you. In case a room becomes available during the night, do you want us to move you or wait until morning? Would you like a sleep mask and earplugs?

I'm sorry. Private rooms are first given to infectious patients, who have first priority for safety reasons. As soon as we do have a room, I promise we will move you.

53

The doctor takes phone calls when he is with me. I think that's rude.

I'm sorry; he always wants to hear what's happening with his patients who are in the hospital. I'll talk with him and ask if I can take messages for him, unless it's an emergency.

I'm sorry that happens. We're completing a list of patient suggestions to improve their visits. May I add your concern to the list?

I'm sorry to hear the phone calls interrupted your visit. Would you like me to ask your doctor if he can stop all calls while he is with you?

54

I'm supposed to learn how to change my mother's dressing, but I am too busy. The nurses will have to do it.

I'm sorry to hear that. How much time do you think you need? If we could show you how to change the dressing in very little time, would you be willing to give it a try? Maybe you are worried you might hurt your mother? Your mother's nurse is an excellent teacher, and I think she could help you get good at this.

I'm sorry; I wish we could always do the dressing change for you. Your mother's benefit plan provides for a certain number of nursing visits structured around the family learning how to do dressing changes when the nurse isn't there. Would anyone else in the family be available to learn? Or would you consider hiring someone to take this on for you?

I'm sorry, and I think I understand how you feel. Other busy families have said they felt the same way about dressing changes. What they have found is that doing the dressing change early in the morning or late at night interferes less in their busy day. I wish I could say we could do all the changes, but that's not possible.

55

The nurse failed to give us information and then yelled at us for not knowing it.

I'm sorry to hear that. It's never fun to be yelled at. Please tell me what happened.

I'm so sorry. Perhaps she thought someone else had told you, but there is no excuse for yelling. Would you like to meet with her to discuss what happened? I can ask her to sit down with us and we can talk about this.

I'm sorry this happened. No one should ever yell at you. What would you like me to do to make this right for you?

56

I watched a nurse sit at the desk and she kept reading while the call bell went off.

I'm sorry to hear that. It's possible another nurse was responding so she kept on with what she was doing.

I'm sorry this upset you. It's hard to know exactly what she was reading, but I can imagine how it looked to you. I'm going to speak with her to let her know she didn't make a good impression.

I'm sorry, and thank you for bringing this to my attention. This morning was extremely busy, and I'm sorry you got a bad impression. Is there anything I can do for you right now?

57

You know, you act like I am an interruption in your day instead of a person who needs help. Do you think I want to be here?

I'm sorry I gave you that impression. I should have stopped what I was doing when you arrived and greeted you. I was too focused on what I was doing. How can I help you now?

You are never an interruption. I'm so sorry you felt that way. I was trying to do too many things at once. You have my undivided attention.

I'm sorry; this has been a very hectic day. I understand this is not the place you'd like to spend your afternoon. I'm all yours now.

58

The doctor forgot about me and left (went to lunch/home/to play golf).

I'm sorry to hear that. I'm sure it was unintentional. Let me page her and find out what we should do.

I'm sorry that happened. You must be upset. Did another doctor take care of you? How can I make this right for you?

I'm so sorry. Would you like to reschedule or should I ask another doctor to see you now? I really do apologize. Your doctor will feel terrible when I tell her this happened. What can I do to help you? Would you like to be the first person to be seen tomorrow morning?

59

I won't pay because your service was so poor.

I'm sorry to hear that. What happened? I'm going to talk with my director, review your care, and see if there is something we can do for you.

I'm sorry. Please explain to me what went wrong. How are you feeling now? If I'm not able to change your bill, is there something else I can do for you?

I'm sorry. I'd like to investigate this situation and call you on Thursday. What's the best time to reach you?

60

The home care aide is lazy.

I'm sorry you've been disappointed. A home health aide's duties are bed making, tidying up, meal preparation, laundry, and helping you bathe and dress. Is your aide doing these things for you? Are there other things you are expecting your aide to do?

I'm sorry to hear that. Please tell me what you mean by lazy. If you want me to, I'll talk with your aide so she understands what your needs are.

I'm sorry. Please tell me more about this so I can figure out how to help you. I want you to be happy with our services.

61

My mother wants to remain as independent as possible with her own personal care and only wants housekeeping assistance. Why can't I get my mother what she wants?

I'm sorry your mother isn't getting what she wants. Can we meet so I can explain what services are approved by her insurance and what services are not? Then she can decide which services to accept.

I'm sorry the home health aide is not able to provide certain services. Perhaps we can help find some other resources for her. There are housekeeping agencies we often recommend in situations like this. I'll talk with your mom to review her options.

I'd like to talk with your mother to understand her reluctance to have the aide help her with personal care. That's what her doctor feels she needs. Sometimes there are alternatives we haven't thought of yet.

I was told that I had to leave because the bed was needed for another patient.

I'm very sorry someone said that to you. That's inappropriate, and I apologize. Would you like to tell me who it was?

I'm sorry someone said that to you. We cannot discharge a patient who is not medically cleared to leave and we won't let you go home unless your doctor says it's time. Let me go check for you.

I'm sorry she upset you; she should not have made that comment. Your doctor has authorized your discharge for today. Do you have your discharge plan? Have we arranged transportation for you? Have all your questions been answered? Are you worried about anything? We'll let you leave only when everything is ready.

63

The last time I came, I was told I was here on the wrong day. Then you blamed me because I had to be squeezed in. And when I got home, the appointment card showed I was right all along.

I'm so sorry. Let me confirm the date and time for your next appointment so we can both be sure I've noted it correctly.

Wow, that must have been upsetting! I'm really sorry that happened to you. I'm glad you were able to be seen that day despite the mix-up. I'm going to make sure you get our very best attention today and every other day you have an appointment.

I apologize. I'm glad you told me. From now on, I'll be more careful.

64

When I asked for something, the nurse embarrassed me in front of my family.

I'm sorry. That should never happen. It might be helpful for you to speak with the Nurse Manager. She could coach the nurse on how to be more respectful.

I'm sorry to hear that. Showing respect for you is very important. The nurse will want to know what she should do differently next time. Please tell me more.

I am so sorry. Is there anything I can say to your family to help in this situation? Would you like me to ask your nurse to come in and talk with you?

65

Everyone complains about how overworked they are because you are short-staffed. Why don't you get more staff?

I'm sorry. They must know you are a good listener, but they shouldn't complain to you.

I'm sorry to hear that. I don't want you to worry. There are hospital requirements about how many staff members are on-duty based on the number of patients we have. We are staffed just right. Is there anything I can do for you right now?

I'm sorry you've been hearing that. I'll remind everyone that we are here to take care of you, not the other way around.

My doctor/nurse doesn't explain things to me.

I'm sorry to hear that, but thank you for telling me. It's very important you know what's happening with your care. I'll alert your doctor to review your care plan and answer all your questions.

I'm sorry. It sounds like you really want to understand your situation better. In order to make the best decisions about your care, you must have all the information you need. Can I prepare a list of your questions? I'll make sure your doctor knows you want to discuss your care and condition.

I'm sorry to hear that. Is there anything you are concerned about right now? I'll take care of that right away and then we'll plan how to get explanations every time you need them.

Everyone keeps asking me the same questions. Don't you write anything down?

I'm sorry. Our doctors and nurses often want to verify your information, so they may ask you questions you have already answered. It is one of the ways we protect your safety. For example, we need to check your identification in two different ways before we give you medication, to be sure it is really for you.

I'm sorry. As a teaching institution, it is customary for each doctor you meet to ask you about your history. It makes for very thorough care even though I appreciate how annoying it can be at times to answer the same questions over and over.

I'm sorry; it can be aggravating, but each person who cares for you wants to think about you and learn about you for themselves. And so they may ask you for information already in your chart. When each person who cares for you knows a lot about you, we think it makes for better care.

68

My mother doesn't speak English. I'm uncomfortable when you make me interpret. Some of your questions are personal and she is a very private person. And I cannot always be there with her.

I'm sorry we've been asking you to interpret. Your mother has the right to her own interpreter. I'll make sure the doctor knows.

I'm sorry. I'll arrange for an interpreter from now on. It's probably a good idea to explain to your mother we are not supposed to use family for interpreting. Why don't you tell her we want to make this change? I'm sorry we didn't do this sooner.

I'm glad you told me. I will personally make sure we have an interpreter here the next time. I'm sorry we have put you in an uncomfortable position.

69

The doctor said I could have the catheter removed. / The doctor said I could be out of bed. / The doctor said I could be on a regular diet. / The doctor said I could have more pain medication. / The doctor said…but nothing is happening.

I'm sorry. It sounds like you're ready to get things going. Let me check your doctor's orders for you. I'll be right back.

I'm so sorry. I know your doctor ordered this and I'll take care of it right now. I'm sorry you had to wait.

That's good news. When did your doctor visit? Your doctor usually writes new orders after he visits all of his patients on the floor unless it's an emergency. I'm sorry you've had to wait.

70

The doctor doesn't listen to me. He's in and out of my room so fast I don't get a chance to say anything or ask my questions.

I'm sorry to hear that. I know it's important for your doctor to listen to you. Would you like me to let him know about this? He may not realize what's happening. I'll leave a note in your chart to let him know you have questions.

I'm sorry you feel this way. I have an idea for you and it usually works. When your doctor comes in and asks how you're doing, you can say, "I have a few questions to ask. Please don't leave until I have asked them."

I'm sorry. Let me help you make a list of the things you want to talk about with your doctor. I'll put a copy on your chart so he'll see the questions before he comes in to see you.

71

The staff didn't care how frightened my child was. There was no effort to calm or reassure her before the procedure.

I'm sorry to hear that. You must have been very upset for your child. What could have been done to reduce her anxiety? What could we have done differently? What has worked for your child in other situations?

I'm so sorry. We want to take very good care of your child. Please tell me more. What can I do to make this better for you and your child right now? Can I help by going over what happened with your child?

I'm sorry we didn't meet her needs or yours. Parents provide some of the best strategies for reassuring children. Can you give us suggestions on how to do this better?

The doctors and staff tell me different things about my condition.

I'm sorry you're hearing different things; that must be upsetting. I'll find out when your doctor is coming and I'll plan to be in the room with you. Could I help you write a list of questions for your doctor to answer?

I'm sorry you're hearing different things. Sometimes we can say the same things in different ways. Let's address your questions one by one and I'll do my best to get each answer for you.

I'm sorry. We want you to be confident about the information we are giving you. Please tell me what you are hearing. I'll look into this, and then we can discuss the details.

73

I'm going home tomorrow and I don't have a clue about what to do when I get there. I don't know if I'll be okay.

Oh my, I'm glad you mentioned this to me and I'm sorry you are so worried. Let me find out what's going on. We'll make sure all of your questions and concerns are answered so you feel confident about going home.

I'm sorry to hear that, but please don't worry. We will write down everything you need to know before you leave. Your social worker will be visiting you today to talk with you about all the details. I'll check with you after that to make sure you feel better.

I'm sorry. We won't let you go until we've had a chance to talk to you about your discharge. We will go over all your discharge instructions to make sure you understand what to do and we'll call you on the next day after discharge to see if you have any questions. Here is my business card. Please call me anytime you need me.

74

My nurse does not understand what I am able and not able to do at home.

I'm sorry. Let's fix this. Can you give me some examples of what she doesn't understand?

I'm sorry to hear that. I'll help you make a list of what you are able to do and not able to do. I'll ask your nurse to go over each item on the list with you. I want you to feel totally confident that you can do all you can, and we will help you where you need it.

I'm sorry you're feeling this way. Your doctor and nurse want you to feel comfortable with what you can do for yourself. Sometimes that feels too hard, and we need to know that so your rehabilitation can go at the right pace. I hear you're getting stronger every day.

75

The staff discriminates against me because I'm on Medicaid/of my race/of my disability/my sexual orientation.

I'm distressed and sorry to hear this. What are we doing that makes you feel this way? What should we stop doing and what should we start doing to show our respect for you? I'll be sure to share your preferences with everyone on your care team.

I'm sorry you feel this way. What can I do to improve this situation for you right now? Let's work together to make this better for you.

I'm so sorry you've experienced this. Respecting the dignity of every person is very, very important to us. What do we need to do differently and what would be the best way for me to raise awareness among my coworkers?

When I visit my mother, she tells me she has to wait a long time for her pain medication.

I'm very sorry to hear your mother has been waiting for her pain medication. We'll fix that right away and I will make sure we do a better job next time. Please encourage her to speak up any time we are not meeting her needs. I'll check back in a little while to make sure the medication is working for her.

I'm sorry. Let's go talk with your mom together to see how we can help her.

Let me confirm how often the doctor has ordered pain medication for her. Then we'll talk together and if she wants, we'll ask her doctor to change the orders.

77

The person who took my blood didn't know what she was doing. She stuck me three times, and when I asked her to use another vein, she didn't listen.

I'm sorry that happened. Would you like me to find out who it was and speak with her manager?

I'm sorry. Let's call the laboratory supervisor and ask that another phlebotomist be sent next time.

I'm sorry you had such a difficult time, but I'm glad you let me know. We don't want you to feel like a pincushion.

I'm in pain and nobody cares. / I'm in agony and no one is taking me seriously. / The pain medicine they give me doesn't work, and they won't call the doctor to get me more! / No one told me that I would be in this much pain. / The IV insertion was painful—she had to stick me four times. / The doctor doesn't believe me about my pain.

I'm sorry to hear you're in pain. How can I make this better for you right now? Would an ice pack help?

I'm sorry you're in a lot of pain. I'll contact your doctor right away. First, please tell me on a scale of 1 to 10, 10 being the worst, how much pain are you feeling right now? OK, I'll be back with an update for you within five minutes.

I'm sorry this is more painful than you expected. Let's see what needs to be done to bring you relief. I'll speak with your care team right away and get back to you.

79

When new staff members begin taking care of me, they don't know how to get me out of the bed without hurting me. My old home care aide knew what to do. She was really careful.

I'm sorry to hear that. I know you were a good team, and I am sure you miss her. I'd like to meet with you and your new worker so we can figure out how to get you out of bed comfortably.

I'm sorry to hear it hurts to get out of bed. Everyone who visits you is highly trained in transferring, because patient safety is very important. I imagine it's scary to have a new person doing something differently. Why don't I ask your old aide to schedule a joint visit with your new aide for a teaching session? I'm sorry we didn't think to do this before.

I'm glad you spoke with me about this. I'll ask the chief therapist to visit you right away for a transfer consultation. We want to make sure everyone who takes care of you knows how you like to get out of bed, and that it is done safely.

I don't want that nurse with the long fingernails to touch me. I'm afraid of her.

I'm sorry to hear that. I understand why you feel this way. Personal grooming is very important and that's why we have standards for all employees. I will see if I can find someone else to care for you.

I'm sorry and I'll have another nurse assigned to you right away. I'll take your concerns to our staff meeting tomorrow and remind everyone that long fingernails are not permissible.

I'm sorry—our dress code specifically prohibits long fingernails. I'm going to report this to our director so she can take corrective action right away.

81

You're finally here, only you've brought the wrong prescription! What are you going to do about this? I can't wait until tomorrow.

I'm sorry. Please give me a moment to check your orders. You're right; this is not the correct medication. I'm very glad you protect your own safety by paying careful attention. I'll correct this today and be back with your medications later.

I'm sorry you think this is the wrong medication. Your doctor has increased the dosage, so this is a different pill, different color and different size. I admire how observant you are because mistakes can happen, and you are the best one to watch for them.

I'm sorry; you are absolutely right. I brought in the next patient's medications by mistake. Her name is very similar to yours. You've taught me an important lesson and I thank you. I'm going to bring in your medications immediately.

82

I don't like all the medicines the doctor has put me on. I don't know what they're for and they make me sick to my stomach. It's just too much to remember and too hard to do.

I'm sorry to hear that. Let's make a list of your medications and you can tell me how you are taking them. We can make a plan together.

I'm sorry to hear that. Your medicine is very important. Has your pharmacist explained your medicines to you? Sometimes how you feel depends on how and when you take your pill. I'll make sure you get all the information you need to feel better.

I'm sorry you are having trouble. Let's talk with your doctor about what you are experiencing. We may be able to help by making some changes.

I was almost given the wrong medication, and no one is telling me about the medicine I'm supposed to be taking. They just hand it to me. No one mentions the side effects either.

I'm sorry to hear that. Tell me what happened. Your safety is very important to us. Let me arrange for someone to visit you to review all of your medications and their side effects.

I'm sorry this happened. Would you like to have a list of the medications ordered for you, and when they are supposed to be taken? We can let you know whether to expect pills, capsules, liquid, or something given by IV.

Our clinical pharmacist will be happy to talk with you to discuss your medications and answer any questions you have. I'm so glad you mentioned this to me. I'm going to call the pharmacy for you right now.

84

I don't get the help I need when I need it. / No one would help me get back to bed. I was in the chair too long. It was torture! / They didn't assist me to go to the bathroom. / No one helped me move off the stretcher/into bed/to the chair. / My visitors had to help me, because the nurse never came. / I was left on the commode for too long.

I'm sorry to hear that. Let's tell your nurse manager together. She wants you to feel we are taking very good care of you. Our job is to make sure you feel comfortable and safe. Or, I can talk with your nurse manager for you and then ask her to come and speak with you.

We should always respond quickly to your personal needs. I will get someone to help you right away.

Let's make sure you can reach your call bell and telephone easily, and they are both working properly. Is there something I can do for you right now? I will stop by more often to make sure you're okay.

85

There have been too many different nurses coming to my home. Some don't know how to do the treatment properly and don't order the right supplies. They are rushed going from one client to the next.

I'm sorry to hear that. To help me understand, I'll pull your records and go over your visits with you. Is this a good time to talk? It's important your care is consistent and your caregivers spend enough time to reassure you.

I'm very sorry. You sound upset and I want to help. Are you okay right now? I will ask your case manager to call you today and review your treatment plan and assigned nurses. We want you to feel you're getting very good care.

I'm sorry your care isn't going smoothly. Your nursing supervisor will make a visit to go over your treatment plan with you. If you give me the days and times this week that are convenient for you, I'll schedule her as quickly as possible.

The technician didn't wear gloves when he took my blood.

This is important to you. If it should happen again, please speak with the technician before he begins. Say: "I'd feel more comfortable if you wear gloves." I'm sure the technician will be happy to reassure you.

I appreciate your concern. Let me find out more about this, and I'll get a box of gloves for you to keep by your bed. Whenever you need them, you can offer them to the technician or anyone else who cares for you.

Would you like to meet the laboratory manager who can discuss our precautions and procedures with you? We're committed to patient safety and we want you to tell us wherever we can improve. Your needs and concerns are very important to us.

87

The doctor/nurse/technician didn't wash her hands.

I'm sorry, but I'm glad that you mentioned this, because we are very strict about handwashing. Although she may have washed her hands before entering your room, it's good you are paying attention.

I'm sorry and I understand your concern. Our staff members are not offended if you ask them about this. I would say something simple such as, "It's really important for me to know you've washed your hands before you take care of me."

I'm sorry to hear that. I'd like to ask one of our infection control professionals to visit you and reassure you about our procedures.

88

The nurse didn't do anything. She took a look around my apartment and left.

I'm sorry to hear that. What were you expecting from the visit today?

I'm sorry. Let me speak with your nurse and check her documentation. I will call you back after I know more. I should have an explanation for you late this afternoon.

I'm sorry to hear that. It's difficult to understand. Did she give you a reason why she was leaving? I will check your orders and review our treatment plan with you to see if there are some answers there. I want to make sure you know what to expect from your nurse and what she should do. Sometimes, the nurse only needs to check on you and not do any treatments, but you should know if that's the case.

The staff wants my family to do their work for them. They're lazy.

I'm sorry to hear that. Often, staff members believe patients feel better when families are involved. However, we never want anyone to feel that they are not receiving the best care. What do you need that we haven't been providing?

I'm sorry; that's not what I like to hear. Although we encourage families to support their loved ones, we don't want them, or you, to feel put upon. When do you expect your family to visit again? It would be good for all of us to talk together.

There are some things that nurses must do, and other things that families or friends can and want to do to help. We encourage that but from what you are saying, we may have overdone it this time. Tell me what happened with your family.

90

You all don't know what you're doing around here! I'm telling everyone I know not to come here.

I'm sorry to hear that. What happened? How can we make this better?

Oh my, I'm sorry to hear that. Your confidence in us is very important. Please help me understand what happened so I can fix it.

We've let you down. You are important to us, so please give me a chance to help.

The resident who comes to see me is too rough. Yesterday, he ripped off my surgical bandage without warning. I'm afraid of what he'll do next.

I'm sorry to hear that. May I share your concerns with him? It's important he knows how you feel.

I'm sorry to hear that. It would be great if you would say something directly to him; I'll be with you, if you'd like. I know the doctor wants you to be comfortable with him and he won't know what happened unless we tell him.

I'm sorry. Sometimes residents are in such a hurry they forget how important a few extra moments can be. I'm sorry about the bandage. I'd like to speak to his supervising physician. Is that okay with you?

92

I don't ever want that person to come to my home again. I don't want (name) taking care of me.

I'm sorry to hear that. Please tell me more. Is there anything she can do to make this right for you? If we can't resolve this, we'll make a change.

I'm sorry to hear you are so unhappy. What happened? Please help me understand what the problem is. It might take a few days to change assignments. Would you rather continue with her until the change is made, or work out something with your family?

I'm sorry; what happened? I'd like to hear about this so I can assign the best person for you. Thank you for telling me.

I can't read my discharge instructions. I can't read what the doctor wrote.

I'm sorry to hear that. Let's call the doctor together and ask what he meant. I can ask him to dictate the note to me and I will write it down for you.

I'm sorry. Let me see if I can translate the instructions for you. I've become an expert in reading your doctor's handwriting. I'll rewrite it for you and remind the doctor to write more legibly next time.

I'm sorry. Let me call the doctor and ask for a printed copy. It shouldn't take long.

94

When I arrived, a nurse said "Enter at your own risk."

Oh, I'm sorry. Her sense of humor can sometimes get her into trouble.

I'm sorry to hear that. We had several emergencies today and she may have been reacting to what happened earlier.

I apologize. That was in bad taste. We had a water main break this morning, but everything's back to normal now.

95

You're still billing me, and I already paid this bill.

I'm sorry to hear that. I'm sure we can fix this quickly.

Sometimes bills and payments cross in the mail. Let's figure this out together. Do you have the bill with you now? Can you read the billing reference number to me? You'll find it in the blue box on the left side.

I'll look into this right away. What's the best number for me to reach you between 3:00 and 4:00 p.m. today? If you don't hear from me by 4:30, please call me. My direct number is _____.

96

I was told my insurance would cover this. Now I have this ridiculous bill. I won't pay it!

I'm sorry. Please let me check on this for you. My department does its best to verify insurance coverage before you have your procedure. I'm just as surprised as you. Let me start with all your details.

I'm sorry; it sounds like we've made a mistake. I will review your entire account and call you back. First, let me check to make sure we have accurate insurance information.

I'm sorry to hear that. Let's take this one step at a time. Have you just received a notice from your insurance company? Would you read it to me and give me the transaction number? If we need to, I will appeal their decision.

You always get my insurance wrong, and I know you're going to screw up this time too.

I'm sorry. Let's check on this right away. What information has been incorrect in the past? Do you have your insurance information with you? I'll make a copy and I promise to make sure your information is correct.

I apologize for the inconvenience this has caused you. I am going to connect you to our Billing Department so they can help, and I will stay on the line with you until everything is straightened out.

I'm sorry. I will refer you to the best person in the Finance Department to make sure it's right. Our insurance expert is (name) and his direct extension is _____. Please call him if he hasn't reached you by mid-afternoon tomorrow.

98

No one told me there was a co-pay for this test. No one told me I had to bring money with me!

I'm sorry to hear that. We should have told you when we made your appointment. When we can't collect the co-pay, we send a bill for the co-pay plus an administrative fee that covers the extra processing we must do for your insurance. I have the authority to waive this fee one time, and I'll be happy to do that for you, if you'd like.

I'm sorry no one told you. We can take your credit card or a check. Which would you prefer?

I'm sorry. Because you don't have a check or credit card with you, we could reschedule your test for another day. Is there someone we could call who would be able to give us your credit card number?

This bill might as well be written in Greek. How the heck am I supposed to know what I owe?

I'm sorry; I'll be happy to help you. I can walk you through the entire statement, or just point out the "amount due now" section.

I'm sorry to hear that. Would you like me to review the information item by item, or did you have questions about only certain parts of the bill?

I'm sorry. I agree; the bills can seem very complicated. I want to be sure the bill is accurate. Do you have time to review it with me now? What ideas do you have about how we can make bills clearer?

You charge too much. It wasn't worth it. Why can't you hold your prices down?

I'm sorry you feel this way. I'll be happy to review the bill with you and try to explain.

I'm sorry. Health care charges have a lot to do with our commitment to having a very high caliber staff, state-of-the-art technology, having staff available 24 hours a day, seven days a week, and compliance with laws and regulations. Would you like our department director to contact you to explain the charges?

I'm sorry. It's now possible to contact us in advance to find out what the charges will be. In the future, when you make your appointment, you can find out how much a test will cost.

101

Why are you sending a collection agency after me? I paid the bill already.

Thank you for telling me. Please give me a moment to look up your account. Oh, I do see a balance due. We might have posted it to the wrong account. Would you be able to send me a copy of your check?

I'm sorry; I will ask someone to look into this immediately. Where can we reach you later today? If you haven't heard from anyone by 4:00 p.m., please call me back. My direct number is _____.

I'm sorry. I'm looking at your account and you do have a zero balance. I will notify the collection agency myself and send you a letter confirming you do not owe us any money. You should have the letter within seven days. Please call me again if you don't receive the letter in that time, or anytime you have questions or concerns. Here is my direct number: _____.

CONCLUSION

From the patient's perspective, a complaint about health care or service is an urgent statement of fact. "I am here where I don't want to be. I am frightened and unsure what will happen next. I put my trust in you, and now something is wrong. How can I be sure I will be okay?" When you respond to a patient's complaint, you are responding to the patient's sense of helplessness and anxiety. The service recovery scripts offered in this book can help you recover a patient's confidence in you and your organization.

We will update *"I'm Sorry to Hear That..." Real-Life Responses to Patients' 101 Most Common Complaints About Health Care* on a regular basis with additional complaints and responses. If you've heard complaints we haven't addressed, or have additional responses to the 101 cited in this book, please send them to susan@susanbaker.com. To express our appreciation, we'll thank you by sending you an electronic copy of our companion brochure—*PI Jumpstarts for Your "I'm Sorry to Hear That..." Complaints.*

We look forward to hearing from you!

Kind regards,

Leslie Bank & Susan Keane Baker

INDEX

ABOUT THE AUTHORS

Susan Keane Baker is the author of *Managing Patient Expectations: The Art of Finding and Keeping Loyal Patients*. She has spoken on service quality for health care organizations and associations in 47 states. Her professional experience includes 17 years in vice president positions at hospitals in New York and Connecticut. For seven years, she directed the Quality Initiatives Program for a national PPO with 19 million members. She is a commissioner on the Connecticut State Commission on Medicolegal Investigations. In 2008, Susan served as a member of the Board of Examiners for the Malcolm Baldrige National Quality Award. Her website is www.susanbaker.com.

Leslie Bank is director of customer service at Montefiore Medical Center, Bronx, New York, a large multi-hospital health care system where a service excellence philosophy is fostered and sustained. She has worked as a "change agent" for over three decades, always aiming at assuring the patient's voice is heard in all aspects of care. Leslie was named "The Mother of Patient-Friendly Billing" after her experience in billing reform following a *New York Times* op-ed entitled "My Golden Hernia." She has authored two commercial customer service videos and has received national awards for patient satisfaction improvement.

ADDITIONAL RESOURCES

Accelerate the momentum of your Healthcare Flywheel®.
Access the list of resources below by visiting a website made just for you:
www.studergroup.com/recovery

Articles:

"Serious About Service" ~Quint Studer
"Making Service Excellence a Priority" ~Quint Studer
"It's Patient Perception of Care — Not a Number" ~Quint Studer
"Infinite Excellence: Live the brand promise by emphasizing 'always.'" ~Lynne Cunningham
"Round Bounty" ~Christine M. Meade

Visit www.studergroup.com/recovery for additional articles that are available.

Books:

Hardwiring Excellence — In *Hardwiring Excellence*, Quint Studer helps health care professionals to rekindle the flame and offers a roadmap to creating and sustaining a culture of service and operational excellence that drives bottom-line results.

What's Right in Health Care: 365 Stories — This 742-page book shares a story a day submitted by your friends and colleagues. It is a daily reminder about why we answered this calling and why we stay with it — to serve a purpose, to do worthwhile work, and to make a difference.

Results That Last — Health care leaders typically read "general business" books and figure out how to apply them to a health care setting. Quint's new book, *Results That Last*, represents a unique opportunity to share the tremendous progress our industry is making with leaders in other business arenas.

Visit www.studergroup.com/recovery for additional books and to view our new books coming soon.

Studer Group® Institutes:

Whether your health care organization is just starting its journey to implementing a culture of excellence or it is looking to create change in a specific area, Studer Group Institutes offer a range of learning opportunities.

Taking You and Your Organization to the Next Level
Learn the tools, tactics, and strategies that are needed to *Take You and Your Organization to the Next Level* at this two-day institute with Quint Studer and Studer Group's Coach Experts. You will walk away with Evidence Based Leadership℠ strategies to create a sustainable culture of execution.

What's Right In Health Care℠
One of the largest health care peer-to-peer learning conferences in the nation, *What's Right in Health Care* brings individuals together to share ideas that have been proven to make health care better.

Visit www.studergroup.com/recovery to view the many other institutes offered by Studer Group.

Speakers:

Author Susan Keane Baker has spoken on service quality for health care organizations and associations in 47 states. To contact Susan about speaking, email her at Susan@susanbaker.com, or for more information, visit her website: www.susanbaker.com.

Coauthor Leslie Bank has been called "The Mother of Patient-Friendly Billing" because of her experience in billing reform and has authored two commercial videos — *Patient Rights: What You Need to Know* and *STAT: A Prescription for Good Patient Relations*. To contact Leslie Bank, email her at lgbank@optonline.net.

Studer Group also provides speaking engagements for health care organizations all over the country. Each speaker has a proven track record with specific knowledge and expertise based on their respective backgrounds.

To learn more about Studer Group national speakers, including the authors of this book, visit www.studergroup.com/recovery.

Learning Videos:

<u>AIDET^{SM} Five Fundamentals of Patient Communication</u>
AIDET—Acknowledge, Introduce, Duration, Explanation, and Thank You—is a powerful communication tool. When interacting with patients, gaining trust is essential for obtaining patient compliance and improving clinical outcomes. AIDET is a comprehensive training tool that will enhance communication within your organization.

<u>Hourly Rounding—Improving Nursing and Patient Care Excellence</u>
A Studer Group Patient Care Model and video/DVD training that contains a key strategy we call hourly rounding. Hourly rounding is not only a call light reduction strategy, but also a proven tactic to reduce patient falls by 50 percent, reduce skin breakdowns by 14 percent, and improve patient satisfaction scores an average of 12 mean points.

<u>Must Haves® Video Series</u>
By implementing the Must Haves, health care organizations around the country are seeing better bottom-line results, including increased volume and decreased length of stay, as well as improved clinical outcomes, staff retention, and recruitment. The Must Haves video series consists of live lectures by Quint Studer, followed by role plays to help organizations hardwire these breakthrough practices into their cultures.

Visit www.studergroup.com/recovery to view additional learning videos.

Magazines:

<u>Hardwired Results Issue 1 Fall 2004</u>
This issue focuses on employee loyalty. Article topics include rounding for outcomes, the power of thank you notes, a case study of Delnor Community Hospital, and a leadership self-test.

<u>Hardwired Results Issue 7 Fall 2006</u>
This issue features articles and tools to drive outcomes. Learn how to improve clinical outcomes with hourly rounding and increase patient satisfaction with individualized patient care.

Visit www.studergroup.com/recovery to view additional *Hardwired Results* magazines.

Webinars:

Studer Group webinars provide the latest information and tools on topics critical to health care leaders. Presented by Quint and other Studer Group coaches, each "on demand" webinar is an hour long. Participants will receive handouts and the opportunity to purchase the webinar on CD to teach other leaders in their organizations.

Visit www.studergroup.com/recovery to learn more about the webinars that are available.

HOW TO ORDER ADDITIONAL COPIES OF

"I'm Sorry to Hear That…"
Real-Life Responses to Patients' 101 Most Common
Complaints About Health Care

Orders may be placed:

Online at: **www.firestarterpublishing.com**

By phone at: 866-354-3473

By mail at: Fire Starter Publishing
913 Gulf Breeze Parkway, Suite 6
Gulf Breeze, FL 32561

(Bulk discounts are available.)

"I'm Sorry to Hear That…"
Real-Life Responses to Patients' 101 Most Common
Complaints About Health Care
is also available online at www.amazon.com.